GOOD CAN COME FROM EVIL

THE STORY OF THE WARRINGTON BOMBING

Written by

Richard Holland

Produced by

The Tim Parry Johnathan Ball Foundation for Peace

in partnership with

Golden Square Shopping Centre

With special thanks to

The Ideas Department

de Winter PR and Marketing

The Peace Centre, Warrington

The Tim Parry Johnathan Ball Foundation for Peace
The Peace Centre, Peace Drive,
Great Sankey, Warrington WA5 1HQ
www.foundation4peace.org

Published by The Peace Centre 2013

Copyright © The Tim Parry Johnathan Ball
Foundation for Peace

ISBN 978-0-9575856-0-7

Printed & bound in Great Britain

by 3LG print ltd, Liverpool

Thanks to the Warrington Guardian for giving
permission to use their images in this book.

All rights reserved. No part of this publication may be
reproduced, stored in a retrieval system, or transmitted,
in any form or by any means, electronic, mechanical,
photocopying, recording or otherwise, without the
prior permission of the publishers.

These views do not necessarily reflect the opinions of any of the
partners involved in making the creation of this book possible.

This book is aimed at children at key stage 2 (7-11yrs). To that end, it has been necessary to simplify language and events in order to enable understanding of what is a complex and difficult situation and set of events. Although the author and publisher have made every effort to ensure that the information in this book is as accurate as possible – it has not been possible to list all events, all parties and all perspectives on the different conflicts referenced in this book. The Foundation therefore advises the reader and those working with, supporting or educating the reader to undertake further research and find out more about people's motivations for becoming involved in violent conflict.

For further information please visit
www.foundation4peace.org
or **email info@foundation4peace.org**

Contents

Foreword by Emma Thompson

I am proud to have been a Patron of The Tim Parry Johnathan Ball Foundation for Peace for ten years, during which time I have been constantly reminded that good did indeed come from the evil inflicted upon so many innocent families in Warrington, and especially the families of Tim Parry and Johnathan Ball.

Twenty years after an IRA bomb killed Tim and Johnathan, I am so proud that the Foundation, named after the boys, has given so much help to other people who have also been hurt by terrorism.

This book has been written, to help the young people of Warrington understand what happened when terrorists bombed the town 20 years ago. It explains how the Foundation, created in memory of the boys by Tim's parents, is now at the very heart of new ways of resolving conflict peacefully.

I hope that the young people who read this book will come to understand the great work which has been done over the last two decades and that it will encourage them to follow our founders' example and help to prevent violence in their own communities and beyond...in the name of peace and reconciliation.

Emma Thompson, Patron
British actress, screenwriter and author.

Good Can Come From Evil

An ordinary day?

It was a Saturday morning in March, the day before Mother's Day. It seemed an ordinary day but it was a day when many people's lives changed forever.

Families were out and about in Warrington town centre helping their children choose cards and presents for the following day. None of them could have imagined what was about to happen.

Two bombs exploded in Bridge Street. Two children were killed and more than fifty people were injured.

The Warrington bombing

The date was March 20th, 1993. Among the busy shoppers in Warrington on that Saturday morning were two boys. Their names were Tim Parry and Johnathan Ball.

Three-year-old Johnathan was in town with his babysitter to buy a Mothers' Day card. Twelve-year-old Tim had already bought his Mum's card and was in a sports shop in Bridge Street buying a new pair of football shorts.

Done Bookmakers where the first bomb exploded

At 12.27pm Tim and his friends heard a loud bang as the first bomb exploded. They ran out of the shop to see what was happening.

The second bomb was hidden in a litter bin next to where Tim was standing and just metres away from Johnathan, who was holding his babysitter's hand. The bombs shattered the bins, sending pieces of metal flying through the air. This shrapnel wounded many people.

Fifty-six people were injured. Johnathan died within an hour of the blast, and Tim was so badly injured, he lost his fight for life five days later.

Witnesses said the scene following the explosions was one of chaos. The air was filled with smoke. Some people were running around trying to find loved ones while others staggered around in shock.

The most seriously injured were taken to Warrington District General Hospital where medical teams worked hard to help those who had been hurt.

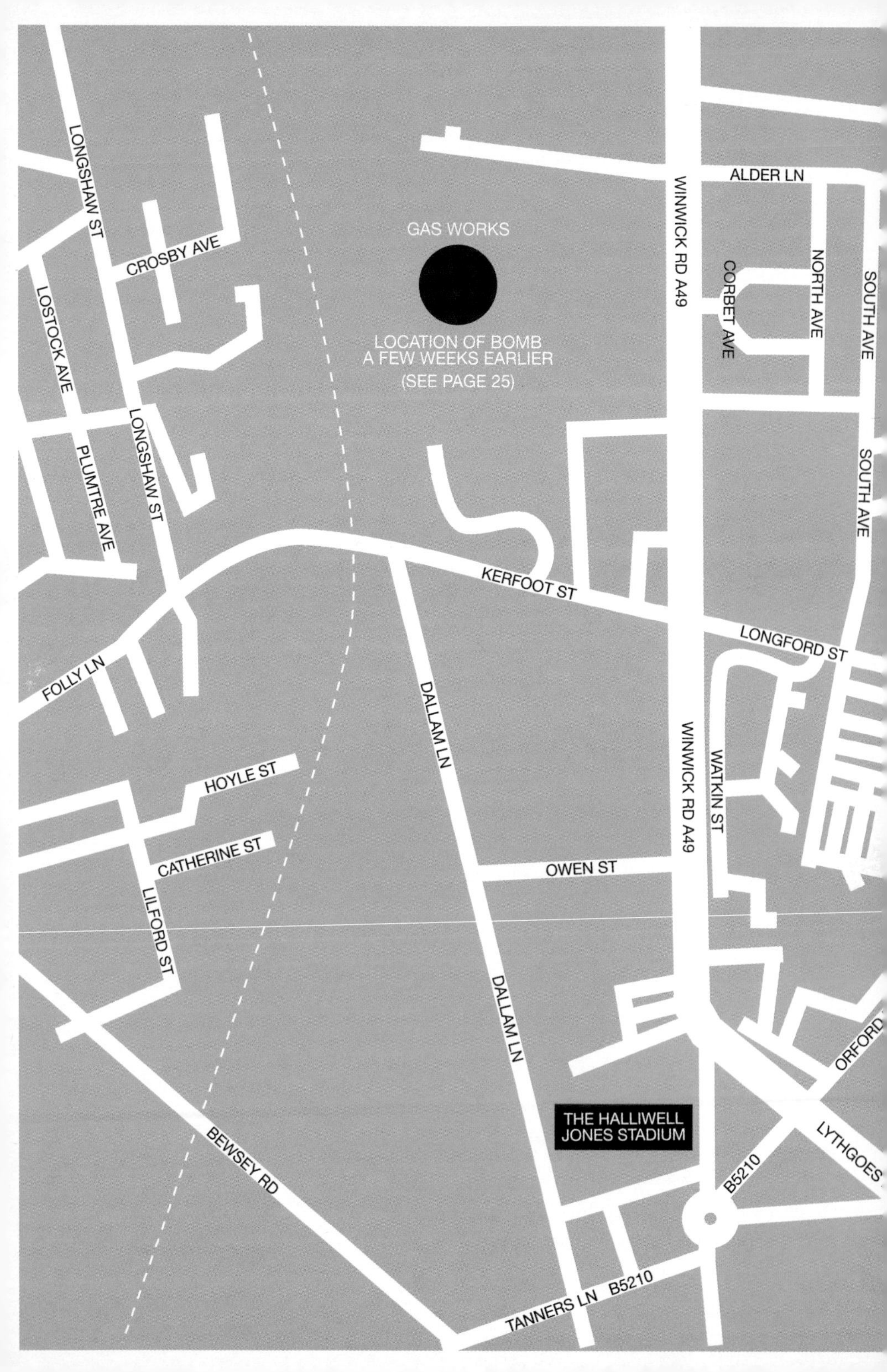
LONGSHAW ST
CROSBY AVE
LOSTOCK AVE
PLUMTRE AVE
LONGSHAW ST
GAS WORKS
LOCATION OF BOMB
A FEW WEEKS EARLIER
(SEE PAGE 25)
ALDER LN
WINWICK RD A49
CORBET AVE
NORTH AVE
SOUTH AVE
SOUTH AVE
KERFOOT ST
LONGFORD ST
FOLLY LN
DALLAM LN
WATKIN ST
WINWICK RD A49
HOYLE ST
CATHERINE ST
OWEN ST
LILFORD ST
DALLAM LN
ORFORD
THE HALLIWELL
JONES STADIUM
LYTHGOES
BEWSEY RD
B5210
TANNERS LN
B5210

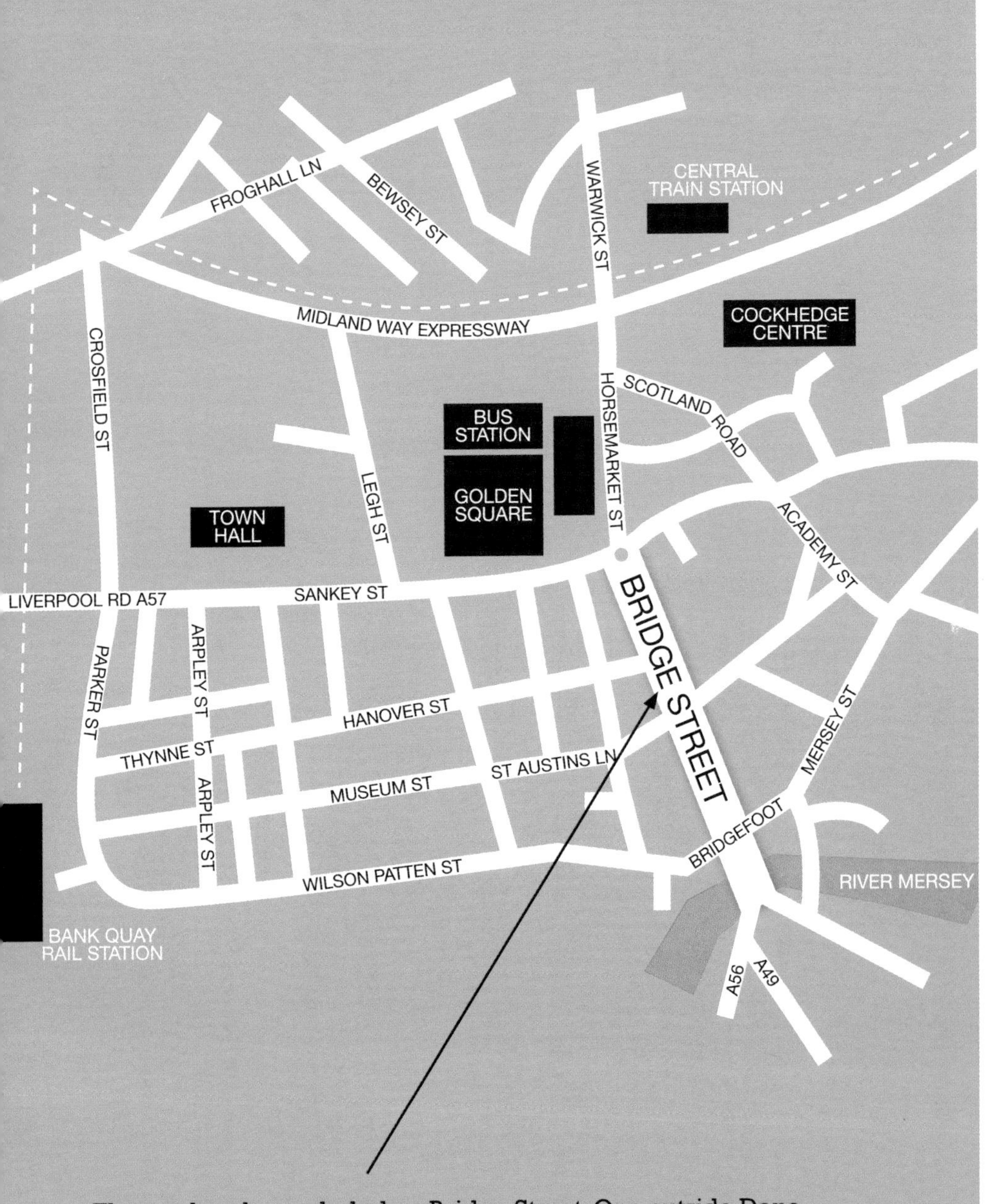

The two bombs exploded on Bridge Street. One outside Done Bookmakers and one outside Boots.

The victims

Johnathan Ball lived in Grappenhall with his mum Marie and dad Wilf. Tim Parry lived in Great Sankey with his mum, Wendy, his dad Colin, his older brother Dominic and his younger sister Abbi.

Tim, like his brother Dominic, went to Great Sankey High School. He was in his first year and was looking forward to all the new and exciting things he would be able to do. He loved football and within a few weeks he was making new friends and playing for the school team.

At the time of the bombing Johnathan was looking forward to his fourth birthday and was very excited about the electric car his dad had bought for him. The fifty-six victims suffered many different injuries. A young couple's legs were so badly hurt they were unable to walk for many months afterwards. A young mother called Bronwen Vickers lost her leg and a year later died of cancer. Many others were hurt and very frightened by what had happened on that day.

United in grief

After the bombing, many people in Warrington were both angry and sad. They wondered why Warrington had been chosen by the bombers, why two young boys had been killed and why fifty-six innocent people had been injured. These questions have never been answered.

On the days of Johnathan's and Tim's funerals the normally busy town of Warrington was very still and very quiet. People were united in grief.

Tim's funeral at St Mary's Church in Great Sankey

Johnathan and Tim were both buried at Fox Covert Cemetery in Appleton, six days apart.

During each funeral procession, crowds of people lined the streets as the funeral cars made their way slowly across town to the cemetery. Children stood silently outside their schools, shopkeepers outside their shops and fire-fighters outside the fire station. Police were stationed at every road junction to make sure other traffic did not stop the procession and each one saluted as the cars went past.

Hundreds of letters, flowers and toys were sent to Warrington for those affected by the bombing and everyone was touched by the love and support they received from strangers.

Tim's friends outside Great Sankey High School

Flowers sent from Tim's football team Penketh United

Terrorism

The bombs were set off by members of a terrorist organisation.

Terrorists use violence and threats against ordinary people as well as those in authority. They also target buildings. They use violence and the threat of violence in an attempt to convince governments to give them what they want.

Terrorism is unusual in this country but it does happen, as it does in other countries all over the world.
On 10th January, 2013, 106 people died and 169 people were injured in two bombings on Alamdar Road in Quetta, Pakistan.

On 7th July 2005 (7/7) bombers attacked three trains and a bus in London killing 52 people.

On September 11th 2001 (9/11) terrorists seized two planes and flew them into the twin towers of the World Trade Center in New York, demolishing the towers and killing thousands of people.

After the attack in New York in 2001, the United States declared a 'War on Terror,' aimed at stopping terrorism all over the world. Sadly, the War on Terror has led to conflict in Afghanistan and Iraq and has led to many people, including children, being hurt or losing their lives.

The War on Terror has not stopped some people from trying to get what they want through violence. Terrorism still affects innocent people in many parts of the world. The Warrington bombing was linked to Northern Ireland. To understand why, it is important to learn about the history of Ireland and its relationship with our own country.

Britain and Ireland

Our country is officially known as the United Kingdom of Great Britain and Northern Ireland. Most people call it Britain or the United Kingdom, often shortened to the UK. Today the UK is made up of England, Wales, Scotland and Northern Ireland. The Republic of Ireland is a separate country and is not part of the UK.

A long time ago, the whole of Ireland was made up of small kingdoms which often fought with each other. In 1171 the King of England, Henry II, sent his armies to invade Ireland. After many battles with the Irish kings he put his own Lord of Ireland in charge.

Hundreds of years later, in 1536, Ireland was invaded again by an English King, this time by Henry VIII. Henry VIII was worried that the latest Lord of Ireland was no longer loyal to him. The Irish were defeated and they agreed to make Henry VIII the King of Ireland as well as of England and Wales.

Flowers and toys left on Bridge Street

Ireland then became part of the United Kingdom for nearly four hundred years and the country was officially called The United Kingdom of Britain and Ireland. However, many Irish people did not want to be part of the United Kingdom. They wanted 'Home Rule' and the right to govern themselves.

Many campaigns were organised over the years to try to persuade the British government to make Ireland a separate country again and to give them their independence. Some of these campaigns were violent and the violence was often met with equal – and at times greater – violence by the British authorities. In the early 1900s the British government began talking about giving back Ireland's independence.

In 1921 an agreement was finally reached and Ireland was separated from the United Kingdom. However, some people didn't want to be separate from Britain and a small part of Ireland voted to stay under British rule. It remained part of the United Kingdom and is called Northern Ireland.

Map of the United Kingdom

The Troubles in Northern Ireland

Some people in Ireland were angry over this compromise, especially in Northern Ireland. They wanted the whole of Ireland to be independent of the UK.

This anger created years of violent disagreement in Northern Ireland, between some of the people who wanted to stay part of the UK (Loyalists) and others who wanted the region to belong to Ireland (Republicans). This ongoing conflict became known as 'The Troubles'.

Among Loyalists and Republicans there were secret societies which used violence to try and get what they wanted in Ireland. Although people knew about the groups, the names of their members were kept secret because of their illegal activities. They would attack soldiers and members of the police force and frighten and sometimes even murder politicians and other important people who disagreed with their goals.

The Irish Republican Army (IRA) was a large Republican organisation fighting for complete separation from Britain. Although the members of the IRA saw themselves as fighting for their country the British and Irish governments saw them as terrorists.

In addition to its other violent activities, the IRA believed it could achieve its goals by frightening and hurting members of the public. Like other terrorist organisations, the IRA believed people would become so frightened they would force their government to do what it wanted. The IRA's campaign of terror included setting off bombs in public places, both in Northern Ireland and in England.

The IRA was responsible for the bombs in Warrington town centre which killed Johnathan and Tim and injured fifty-six people.

Mural in Northern Ireland 'Lest We Forget'

Why Warrington?

In February, 1993, a few weeks before the bombings in Bridge Street, a gasworks in Warrington was attacked by the IRA. They tried to blow up large gas containers. This caused a large explosion which could have injured and possibly killed many people. Luckily the attack failed, although a policeman was shot and injured when he investigated the terrorists' getaway vehicle.

Four members of the IRA were caught and jailed for their part in the attempt to blow up the gasworks. Some people believe the bombing in Bridge Street three weeks later was revenge for the arrests.

No warning

The IRA had made a promise to warn the authorities before setting off bombs in public places. It would do this by giving two identical warnings within minutes of each other. A code-word would also be provided to prove the threat was a real one, not a hoax.

On 20th March 1993, only one warning was given and it was given to the Samaritans in Liverpool. Worse still, the warning said that a bomb had been placed outside a Boots store but didn't say in which town.

Even though the code that the IRA gave was wrong and the police had good reason to believe the warning was a hoax, they acted quickly and cleared Liverpool city centre of shoppers. They searched for the bomb they believed might be hidden there. When they couldn't find it, they told the police in nearby towns, but just as the police in Warrington received this warning, the first bomb in Bridge Street exploded. The second bomb exploded seconds later.

32p

WARRINGTON GUARDIAN

2PM SPECIAL EDITION

ABC

TEL: 33033 YOUR LOCAL FAMILY NEWSPAPER SINCE 1853 Friday, February 26, 1993

IRA assassins target Warrington in night of horror

TERROR ON THE STREETS

INSIDE

Eye-witness accounts of police shooting
- Pages 6-7

Back to the Blitz
How the chaos of war returned to Warrington
- Pages 2-3

One blast and then panic
- Pages 4-5

Deserted ... Warrington's Sankey Street shopping centre is cordoned off after the IRA terrorist attack on the town's Winwick Road gas works which caused a huge fireball, inset, at 4.00am. today.

Warrington Guardian Newspaper

Memorials to the victims

In October, 1993, Warrington Borough Council put up a plaque as a memorial to the two boys killed by the IRA bomb attack. It was placed on the wall of the Boots the Chemist shop in Bridge Street, very close to where the second bomb exploded. Johnathan and Tim's smiling faces are shown on the plaque to remind everybody of the two young lives that were lost.

The plaque was unveiled by Tim's mum Wendy Parry and Johnathan's mum Marie Comerford in front of hundreds of people who came to remember the boys.

Three years later a much larger memorial called the 'River of Life' was constructed in Bridge Street to remember Tim and Johnathan and the other fifty-six victims. It was designed by an artist with the help of students from the school that Tim attended.

The artist also worked with children from local primary schools to create the discs running down Bridge Street which tell the story of Warrington's history and environment.

On November 14, 1996, the 'River of Life' was officially opened by a member of the Royal Family, The Duchess of Kent.

Johnathan's and Tim's mums unveiling the Plaque on Bridge Street

River of Life. A memorial to all the victims of the Warrington bombing

Support from around the world

The deaths of Johnathan and Tim shocked the world and a message came from the then President of the United States, Bill Clinton, who wrote:

'Let me join the people of Warrington in extending my deepest sympathy to the victims of the recent bombing and their families. My prayers are with them and all other victims of the wave of terrorist violence.

'The American people join the people of Ireland and the United Kingdom in expressing their sympathy to those touched by these outrages, in believing that violence from whatever quarter can never be justified, and in hoping that out of this tragedy will emerge a new determination to seek peace and reconciliation through dialogue.'

Sympathy in Ireland and Northern Ireland

People in Ireland were also saddened by the Warrington bombings. In Dublin, the capital of the Republic of Ireland, 20,000 people gathered to show their anger at the attack. Some of them marched under a banner which said 'Enough is Enough'.

Some people in Northern Ireland were upset and angry about what had happened and they wanted everyone to know that they did not agree with what the IRA had done. New campaigns were launched to try and convince both Republican and Loyalist terrorists in Northern Ireland to stop the violence.

The Irish community in Warrington showed support for the victims and their families and spoke about their disgust at the people who had planted the bombs. But because the bombers had come from Ireland, a lot of anger was turned on Irish people living in Warrington. In the weeks following the tragedy, the Irish Club in Warrington suffered vandalism, including having its windows broken.

20,000 people gather in Dublin, Ireland to say 'Enough is Enough'

Other attacks

For a few years the calls for peace from around the world were ignored and the violence in Northern Ireland continued. More people died.

On April 24th 1993, the IRA set off a bomb in London. This time a correct warning was given to the police. Although the police did their best to clear the area, one person died and more than forty others were injured by the explosion.

Another seven people were hurt on July 6th when an IRA bomb exploded in the Northern Ireland town of Newtownards.

Loyalist terrorist groups also carried out attacks. On October 6th, 1993, the Ulster Freedom Fighters killed one person and injured two others in a shooting in Belfast. On the same day the Ulster Volunteer Force set off a bomb outside a Republican political party office in Belfast.

On October 23rd a bomb was set off in a fish shop in Belfast. The IRA believed Loyalist terrorists were going to use a room above the shop for a meeting but the bomb went off too soon, killing an IRA member, a member of a Loyalist terrorist group and eight people who happened to be in the shop.

In revenge Loyalist terrorists with guns went to a pub where they believed IRA supporters were gathered and fired into the crowd. Eight people were killed and thirteen wounded.

These were among the last acts of violence carried out by Northern Irish terrorists. In 1994 the IRA declared a ceasefire. They agreed to no longer carry out violent acts, provided Loyalist terrorists did the same. The Loyalists agreed.

The ceasefire lasted until 1996 but after disagreements, bomb attacks started up again. Fortunately, after more talks, another ceasefire was called a year later.

Today both sides are continuing to work towards a solution to their differences without violence.

Weapons have been destroyed so they can never be used again. The ceasefire is still in place although there are some people who remain unhappy with the outcome and some acts of violence have taken place in Northern Ireland.

A 'living memorial'

In 1993 Tim's mum and dad, Wendy and Colin Parry, were taken to Northern Ireland by the BBC in order to make a TV documentary programme. They talked with people who hated violence and some who, like them, had lost loved ones in terrorist attacks. They also met people who believed violent acts were needed to get what they wanted.

One place they visited really inspired them. This was the Peace Farm in Coleraine, Northern Ireland. The farm was in the countryside which provided a safe place for young people to meet and talk about 'The Troubles'. The teenagers Colin and Wendy met came from all over Northern Ireland and had very different views. However, they all believed that a peaceful solution could be found.

Three of the young people had family members who were killed by terrorists but they did not want revenge – they just wanted peace so that no one else would suffer like they had. After losing their son in the same way, Colin and Wendy were impressed by their views.

The Peace Farm made them think how good it would be to set up something similar in Tim's and Johnathan's names. An ongoing project about peace and understanding would be the perfect way to make sure they weren't forgotten and that some good could come out of their deaths.

The project would be a 'living memorial' to the two boys.

The Foundation for Peace

In April 1995, an important event happened: the Tim Parry Johnathan Ball Foundation for Peace was launched.

The charity was created in memory of the boys to help promote the understanding and resolution of conflict. Work began straight away by bringing together eight teenagers from Warrington, eight from the Republic of Ireland and eight from Northern Ireland. In a quiet place in the Irish countryside the young people got to know each other and talked about 'The Troubles'.

One of the first groups from Warrington were pupils from Tim Parry's school, Great Sankey High. The fact they knew one of the victims personally had a big effect on the Irish young people. It helped them to see the victims of terrorist attacks as real people, with friends and family who loved them – not just as photographs in the newspaper. The experience also helped the Great Sankey pupils to understand the situation in Ireland, and to realise that most Irish people did not support the violence.

The visits were so successful that Colin and Wendy were soon asked if Irish teenagers could visit Warrington. After being so inspired by the Peace Farm, Wendy suggested they could build a 'Peace Centre' in Warrington which could be dedicated to the boys.

The Peace Centre

One of the many people Colin and Wendy talked to about the fundraising was an important politician called Mo Mowlam, who was the British government's Secretary of State for Northern Ireland. This means she was involved in making decisions about how Northern Ireland should be run. Mo also arranged talks between the IRA and Loyalist terrorist groups and her work helped to bring peace to Northern Ireland.

Mo Mowlam agreed that a Peace Centre in Warrington was a great idea and she encouraged Colin and Wendy to go ahead. Through many acts of generosity, enough money was soon raised to build the Peace Centre.

The Peace Centre was opened exactly seven years after the Warrington bombings, on March 20th, 2000. It was officially opened by the Duchess of Kent, who had opened the River of Life memorial a few years earlier. The building was designed so that from the air its shape looks a bit like a flying dove, which is a symbol of peace.

The Peace Centre built in memory of Tim and Johnathan

Good from evil

The terrorist bomb attack on Warrington in 1993 shocked the world. Two children were killed and fifty-six people were injured, including Bronwen Vickers who died the following year.

Some people were very angry, but even more felt worried for the victims and wanted to make sure nothing like this ever happened again.

New efforts to end the conflict in Northern Ireland were made by politicians in Britain and Ireland. After hundreds of years of violence, some peace did come to Northern Ireland. People are still working hard to find a permanent solution to their disagreements.

In Warrington the Tim Parry Johnathan Ball Foundation for Peace was set up in the names of the two boys killed by the bombs.

The Foundation for Peace has supported and helped thousands of people affected by terrorism, helped thousands more by giving them the skills they need to end conflict in their own communities, and it has built the Peace Centre in memory of the boys.

Nothing can bring Tim or Johnathan back. But their names live on in the best way possible: as symbols of peace and of hope.

At Tim's funeral his father Colin said he believed that good could come from evil.

With the hard work of the Tim Parry Johnathan Ball Foundation for Peace and the support and kindness of people from all over the world, a great deal of good has come out of an act of evil.

Glossary

Injured. When a person's body has been damaged in an accident or by an act of violence. Injuries can be minor, such as cuts and bruises, or more serious, such as broken bones. Injuries can be so serious they cause a person's death.

Shrapnel. Bits of metal which can be sent flying out at great speed from an exploding bomb. Shrapnel often causes more injuries and deaths than the force of the explosion itself.

Terrorist. A terrorist is someone who tries to change attitudes or the way things are run by using violence and threats against ordinary people as well as people in authority. They believe that by making people terrified, they will get what they want.

Officially. Formally agreed on or recognised by people in authority.

Invade. When one country sends its army across the border into another country with the intention of taking control of it.

Home Rule. The right for the people of a country to govern themselves.

Govern. To run a country through laws and regulations with the support of its people. A Government is a body of people who have been put in charge of running a country.

Authorities. The people in charge. This includes the Government and in some cases the Police Force or Army.

Compromise. A compromise is a solution which everyone can agree on. A compromise will not give either side in a disagreement exactly what they want but will satisfy them enough to end the conflict.

Loyalists. People who want Northern Ireland to stay part of the United Kingdom.

Republicans. People who want Northern Ireland to leave the United Kingdom and become part of the Republic of Ireland instead.

Conflict. Violent disagreement between two or more people or groups of people.

'The Troubles'. A name given to the violence which took place in Northern Ireland between Loyalists and Republicans from the 1960s to the 1990s.

Hoax. Pretending something has happened when it hasn't. A hoax can just be a joke but some can have serious consequences, such as hoax calls to the police or to the fire service.

Memorial. Something set up to remember people or an event. Memorials can include an object like a plaque, statue or building; a charity or other organisation; or an activity that regularly takes place.

Ceasefire. A call to stop fighting. This can mean the end of a war or it might be just a period when the fighting stops while talks to end the conflict are taking place.

Resolution. A firm decision to, for example, end a conflict or disagreement. The peaceful solution found to end that conflict.

Afterword

Since the Warrington bombing and losing Tim, Colin and I have devoted our lives to developing the Foundation, building the Peace Centre and helping those whose lives have been changed forever through acts of terrorism and conflict. We hope that our efforts have made a difference to people's lives and they are able to take what they have learnt back into their own communities.

This book proves that hope can come from evil, that conflict can be resolved by non-violent means and, for the Parry and Ball families, a way of remembering Tim and Johnathan's bright smiling faces full of hope.

Wendy and Colin Parry.

Index

Index